GOD PRESENT

GOD PRESENT

By Georges Lefebvre, O.S.B.

Translated by the Rev. John Otto
in collaboration with
Marie Philip Haley, C.S.J.
Mary Virginia Micka, C.S.J.

Originally published in France under the title
Dieu présent
Copyright © 1978 Desclée de Brouwer

Copyright © 1979 by Winston Press, Inc.
Library of Congress Catalog Card Number: 79-64653
ISBN: 0-03-053436-4

Designed by Nancy Arend

5 4 3 2 1

Winston Press
430 Oak Grove
Minneapolis, MN 55403

ACKNOWLEDGMENTS AND PERMISSIONS

Other books by Georges Lefebvre

Simplicity: The Heart of Prayer
Courage to Pray (in collaboration with Anthony Bloom)

TABLE OF CONTENTS

Father Georges Lefebvre's small, simple book is full of the vision of peace—peace to be found in the presence of God under the loving gaze of him who from the beginning, through word and sign, has been present to his creation, acting to draw us all into a life-giving union with himself.

Our faith-filled response to this call, together and individually, is both our history and our prayer: a response in utter and complete simplicity translates our belief into our prayer. What results from recognizing the interdependence of these two aspects of religion will become the rich and gracious experience of readers of this book.

Father Lefebvre has developed these insights in two sections. The first is a clear, essential theology of God's indwelling presence in human history, in the person of Christ, in the community of believers and in the individual Christian. The second carries this theology beyond discussion to personal prayer. Here paragraph and sentence give way to simple phrases, phrases open on spaces, to provide a kind of visual transition into the profound and unutterable response of the heart before the reality of this indwelling presence.

Such a book, such a format, supports the contemporary search for an individual, personal prayer that is both rooted and free; used by small prayer groups, it could help foster this experience in community.

Marie Philip Haley, C.S.J.
Mary Virginia Micka, C.S.J.
Still Water House of Prayer
Stillwater, Minnesota
Summer, 1979

Prayer, simply speaking, means living the presence of God: a presence that reaches to the center of our being and at the same time wraps us round; a presence living in the depths of our heart but also felt in the humblest actions of life. The many aspects of this presence are expressed by the various affirmations of our Christian faith, all of which converge in the reality at the heart of this mystery—the Incarnation: God entering into and dwelling within our history.

If we are to grasp the full meaning of our prayer, we must ponder the mystery of the Incarnation: Christ's presence in human history and his continued presence under the sign of the Church. Only in this perspective can we understand the deepest dimension of our prayer and the power of grace on which it rests.

What great nation is there that has its gods so near as Yahweh our God is to us whenever we call to him? *Deut. 4:7*

Chapter 1

THE GOD OF HISTORY

The God who reveals himself to us in sacred scripture is a God who is present.

In human life we reveal ourselves not so much by definition as by our actions: our way of doing and saying things becomes our manner of manifesting ourselves, of being present, to one another. Something like this happens in biblical revelation: God reveals his presence as a personal God by freely making a covenant of love and grace with the people he had chosen and through them with all humankind.

Throughout the Old Testament God draws his people to an ever greater awareness of his love. Again and again the prophets remind Israel of this love of predilection on the part of God, who has taken Israel for his people forever and has become their God (Exod. 6:7). Hosea expresses this love in language of incomparable human tenderness: "I myself taught Ephraim to walk, I took them in my arms; yet they have not understood that I was the one looking after them. I led them with reins of kindness, with leading-strings of love. I was like someone who lifts an infant close against his cheek; stooping down to him I gave him his food" (11:3-4).

It was a long time before other nations were brought to the revelation of this great mystery of a God calling his creation into a relationship of love with himself. First the chosen people had to become aware of this love of predilection, to recognize themselves as loved by a God who had chosen them from among all peoples and guided them step by step through their history; then they had to learn that they were called not only to respond to this love but also to give witness to it before all nations.

Only with the coming of Christ, however, do we have the full revelation of this presence of love, the love of a God who wants to be infinitely near to all of us, present in our total history in order to uphold it by his grace and bring us all to full intimacy with him.

These then are the two closely related aspects of the mystery revealed to us in Christ:

The fullness of the love with which God loves us.

The reality of his presence in human history.

I want those you have given me to be with me where I am. I have made your name known to them and will continue to make it known, so that the love with which you loved me may be in them, and so that I may be in them. John 17:24,26

Chapter 2

THE REVELATION OF LOVE

With the coming of the One who called himself the Son of God, the only Son of the Father, God-with-us—with that event everything is changed. Continuity with the past is not interrupted—continuity, that is, with the long tradition of covenant relationship which prepared Israel to receive this ultimate testimony of God's love. But at the same time everything is made new. The new covenant that God forms with all people, the relationship he offers to each of us in the heart of this covenant, truly heralds the "new age," when the Kingdom of God is literally in our midst and is expressed in words we had never heard before.

"As I, who am sent by the living Father, myself draw life from the Father, so whoever eats me will draw life from me" (John 6:57).

"Father, may they be one in us, as you are in me and I am in you. . . . That the love with which you loved me may be in them, and so that I may be in them" (John 17:21,26).

In Christ there is above all the revelation of God's hidden inner life, the life of the Three-in-One. When Christ speaks of the union he enjoys with his Father, he always speaks of it in relation to the union he, Christ, wants us to have with and in himself; and indeed it is only in the light of this revelation that we can know, even dimly, the depths of the intimacy into which God draws us. Christ's words unfold a mystery beyond our ability to imagine, revealing as they do not only the mystery of God's innermost life but, what is more awesome, his desire to have us share in it so intimately that we experience a real participation in his life, a real entering into the communion of love that is the very life of the Trinity itself.

Christ reveals that God is not a solitary sovereign who rules his creation from afar. Such a God could not love. He could be good, benevolent, but he could not love because there would be no object worthy of his love, no object in which his love could rest, no person with whom to create a bond of love. The revelation of God in Christ is one of a God not alone but existing in a communion of love triune and personal, binding Father and Son in the Spirit. These divine Persons are all that they are in the unity of one divine nature—a unity they live in an exchange of love.

It is Christ who reveals this mystery of the trinitarian communion, the mystery of a God who because he himself is a communion of love can also introduce us into the communion of love that is his very life. This he does in Christ. In making us one with his only Son the Father loves us with the love by which he loves the Son. He gives us his Spirit, in whom he loves us with the love by which he loves his Son. And by the Spirit he gives us the power to love him in and with his Son with a truly filial love. It is in and with Christ that we are called to live this union by being in and with him children of the Father, living the divine sonship he has come to share with us. In and with him we enter into the mystery of unity that characterizes the trinitarian life. For there is only one love in God and it is by this love that we are loved when we become in the Son children of the Father.

Only a God incarnate could reveal such a mystery and make it believable. Only by his taking on our human condition can we possibly believe he wants us to take on his divinity. For indeed why would he have assumed our condition if not to give us a share in his? Or how could he have gone to such an extreme of love, making himself one of us, if not in order to admit us to true intimacy with himself? And we, would we have been completely one with him had he not first become one of us?

The divine Persons do not exist anterior to the relationship that unites them. All that they are they are in and through this relationship. Similarly, we exist in and through a relationship to God, from whom we receive everything in a communion of love, our communion of love with his Son. The only thing God cannot give us is the power to possess something as our own, as belonging to us, as having been received from ourselves. It follows that we who are as nothing before him cannot live the communion he invites us to live except in wonder, akin to worship, at a love that can give itself so intimately and draw us so near to him. Our communion with God calls us to an absolute humility in his presence.

Clearly this attitude of humility is a condition—or rather, a characteristic of love. For if love is full communion, we can enter it only when we no longer have anything of our own; for whatever we try to keep as our own we withhold from this communion. In the image of the divine Persons, therefore, who themselves hold nothing except in an exchange and communion of love, we too are called to the total and absolute emptying of self essential to love. In order to be all that we are in this communion we are called to accept the essential poverty, the essential humility, required of love.

For love is more than a feeling of attraction. It is the firm will to be all that we are in intimate union with the other, to be bound as a whole person with the one for whom, in order to exist, we have greater need than for ourselves. Such a bond one cannot forge except by committing oneself entirely, with all that one is, to a new manner of being oneself: existing and living in a union in, by and for the sake of which one is all that one is; for we recognize that we can no longer truly exist, truly live, except insofar as we bring all that we are into this common partnership, this loving communion with the other.

In all this, however, God does not simply ask that we be humble "before" him, aware of our nothingness in the presence of his infinity. Rather, he asks that we be humble "with" him; that "with" him we live that humility of love that is dispossession of self, non-belonging to self because no longer capable of existing except in communion with the other; that "with" him we find in this communion our only good, our only happiness, recognizing now our need of the other in order to live.

Such is the essential revelation found in Christ, the revelation of love. When the Son of God came into the world, this love was confirmed by the utterly new relationship that came into being between God and humankind. In Christ and through him we learn how profound is this intimacy we are called to live and at the same time how profound is the secret of the trinitarian life that makes possible such intimacy between God and his humble creature.

And know that I am with you always; yes, to the end of time.
Matthew 28:20

Chapter 3

THE REVELATION OF A PRESENCE

The great Sacrament

Christ is God-with-us, Emmanuel. As such he is the Sacrament *par excellence*, the great Sacrament. He is not only the sign but the reality of the union between God and humankind in the person of Christ. He is the sign and the reality of the love God shows by coming to us in this way. Furthermore, by this unprecedented act God not only reveals how great is the intimacy he wants us to have with him but what is more, makes it possible for us to believe him. For as St. Leo the Great has observed, it is indeed "less astonishing to see a human being raised to the divine than to see God lowering himself to humanity" (Sermon 24, Fourth on the Nativity).

The Old Testament records a period of preparation during which God gradually revealed himself through his interventions in the history of his people Israel. The Incarnation, when God entered our history as a human being, was the act by which he revealed fully and definitively his great love for us and his desire to be near us.

For through the Incarnation the presence of God in human history—an essential characteristic of all biblical revelation—became a new reality. In and through the humanity of Christ God himself not only intervened in this history but as a man entered into and acted within it. Thus in the fidelity of his love God formed in and through Christ a true solidarity with human history, wherein the work of Christ moves forward now toward the fulfillment he alone can bring it to.

God could not have meant such a bond with his creation to be merely a passing reality limited to the few years Christ spent on earth with us. Instead, Christ's coming radically and definitively changed the relationship between God and his creation, thus marking the beginning of a whole "new age."

In this light the Ascension can be understood not as the departure of Christ in the sense that by returning to his Father he ceased to be with us, but rather as the beginning of a new mode of presence of Christ in our history, a presence new but no less real. For history now no longer exists except in him, moving to fulfillment only in him, borne along in the grace of his presence.

The sacrament of the Sacrament

Since the Ascension Christ remains present in our history through the invisible action of his Spirit. He himself said that it was necessary for him to "go away," necessary that his visible presence among his disciples come to an end so that another mode of presence could be realized. But he indicated that this new mode of presence through the Holy Spirit would surpass the former: "Nevertheless I tell you the truth: it is to your advantage that I go away, for if I do not go away, the Counselor will not come to you; but if I go, I will send him to you" (John 16:7).

This new presence of Christ through the Holy Spirit would not be completely invisible, however. At the moment when he commissioned his apostles to make disciples of all nations he promised to remain with them, saying, "And know that I am with you always, to the end of time" (Matthew 28:20). These words echo the same firm promise of the other declaration, addressed to Peter: "You are Peter, and on this rock I will build my church" (Matthew 16:18). If Peter is the Rock, the foundation of the Church, it is because Christ is with him, for the Church can be built on no other foundation than Christ.

This promise of Christ to remain with his apostles to the end of time makes of them *signs* of his presence in his Church—and not only them but all to whom they were to pass on this mission in his name. Herein also is clarified the meaning of priesthood in the Church. It is by reason of a mission received from Christ and only from him that the priest in the exercise of priesthood signifies sacramentally that Christ is ever present and acting in his Church. It is from Christ alone that the Church receives—and never ceases to receive—its all. It is Christ who teaches the Church, sanctifies it, governs it through those entrusted by him with the mission of ministering in his name; and it is from him alone that this commission can be received to be "clear and visible signs of him who is invisibly present among us."[1]

But the promise of Christ to be present in his apostles extends to all the Church carried along and supported by his sacramental presence. The whole of the Christian community is a sacramental sign under which Christ remains present in history, a sign that is also a part of history. The whole community of believers, animated by the Spirit of Christ, vivified by his presence, bears witness to the world that Christ is always present, living and acting at the heart of our history.

This clarifies our understanding of the nature and function of the Church as a *sign*, a sign that gives way before the presence it signifies: the presence of Christ truly inserted in our history, a presence ever actual, near at hand and accessible; a presence manifesting itself as ever acting under the signs given us.

It is in and through the Church that we understand the plenitude of the mystery of God's definitive entering and involvement in our history—a history he sustains and draws to fulfillment by the very grace of his presence. Because this mystery of the Incarnation lies at the heart of our faith, because in it alone rests our hope, revealing as it does the extent of God's love for us and making this love believable, we cherish and draw close to the sacrament of the Church, wherein his presence among us abides under sacramental signs.

The sacraments

The sacraments are the focal points of this presence of Christ in the Church. He has given us these signs with the promise that every time they are enacted in his name he will be present in them and will act through them.

Thus each time we receive a sacrament we come to an encounter with Christ, who draws our whole being into the mystery of his Incarnation. Furthermore, as in daily life we create special times to celebrate and nourish the bonds of intimacy among our family and friends, so do the sacraments become for us times and means of meeting Christ, of celebrating and strengthening his presence in our lives. Filled as they are with the grace of his presence they provide for our very human need to come together with those we love in order to express and nurture an abiding intimacy that is the joy of our every day.

But sacraments are not only a grace for each person who receives them. They are above all signs of Christ's presence acting in history to bring his work of salvation to universal fulfillment.

We have said that God reveals himself in our history. He intervened in it throughout the long period of preparation and since Christ's coming has identified himself with it once for all.

Just as the "events" recorded in sacred scripture were acts of God, so do the sacraments continue the interventions of God in history; they are true "events" in the biblical sense. Through them God is continually manifesting himself as the God of history; through these signs of his presence, the gift of his love for us, he is accomplishing his saving work.

The sacraments remind us again that, like the Old Testament revelation of God's active presence in the history of Israel, the New Testament Christian revelation is also more than a set of abstract truths dictating a certain rule of life to which our actions are to conform. That kind of thinking would indeed soon reduce "religion" to nothing more than "morality." The essence of Christian revelation, as St. Paul so often reminds us, is "mystery," the very mystery of God's life, the plan and purpose of which is incarnated in Christ. In and through Christ this mystery becomes concrete, human, flesh and blood, present at the very heart-center of our world, giving "religion" an entirely new meaning.

Our prayer is intimately bound up with the mystery of this new presence: on the one hand its grace carries our prayer along, and on the other, prayer enables us to live it fully. But could we so intensely live this presence, so often hidden, were there no sign to recall it; no sign to strengthen our faith; above all, no meeting with Christ in what is for us the sacrament of sacraments, the Eucharist? For this meeting with Christ in the Eucharist, especially if it is frequent, heightens as nothing else can our awareness of our life with him. Indeed in moments when it becomes difficult for us to find Christ in prayer the sacrament of the Eucharist can be an unfailing support to our faith, the sign he has given us, a sign carrying in itself the grace to recognize him in it if we but trust in his word.

Our deepest prayer arises out of our union with the presence of Christ within us, a presence we encounter preeminently in the Eucharist, but also in all the other sacramental signs of his saving presence in the Church and, through the Church, in the world. This is the mystery we live, in communion with Christ always present and acting in his body the Church, a body become through him a bearer of grace to all of humankind.

The church of the living God, pillar and bulwark of truth.

1 Timothy 3:15

Chapter 4

THE ACCEPTANCE OF FAITH

The mystery of a God who invites all humankind to a covenant of love was revealed in the history of Israel, the people of God. By sharing in the faith of the community who first received this revelation we ourselves receive the message addressed to them and open ourselves to the grace of the mystery shown forth in their lives.

Similarly, it is within the Church that the new community of God receive and are sustained in faith, a faith enabling them to enter as a people into a deeply personal bond with him: "It is as one body that Christians live together in faith. The certitude of faith is a certitude held in common. This faith of the Church, the fruit of the Holy Spirit abiding in it, enables the Christian struggling through spiritual drought and darkness to be restored to life little by little by breathing, so to speak, the faith of others. One of the most joyful realities of the spiritual life is this very community of faith and the mutual solidarity it implies for Christians."[2]

To understand how deeply grounded is this solidarity we must remember that faith does not lie in adhering simply to abstract truths. It is primarily adhering to a person, Christ. It is living out a wholehearted engagement of our entire being with the One in whom we have placed our faith.

Sharing in the faith of the Church means sharing in the entire life of the Church. It means sharing in the life of all Christians who from generation to generation have received the message of salvation and by living it have increased their understanding of its inexhaustible truth. This deepened "sense of faith" which we in turn receive illumines for us the profundities that still lie hidden but that our own lives will make clearer for the Christians who come after us. The message of faith transmitted to us in the Church is thus truly a living word.

This word wherein God expresses and reveals himself he first spoke in the course of Israel's history. From the center of the life of this people, from the heart of their tradition, emerged the consciousness of being chosen by God, loved by him with a love of predilection. But the full meaning of this election became apparent only when God himself came to earth to take part in our history and in so doing to give it a new meaning that surpassed all the expectations of Israel.

These divine interventions are recorded in the scriptures, but their message of salvation remains actively interwoven in the history of a people who continue by their lives to transmit it. The Christian's faith rests on the testimony of the apostles, who saw Christ and to whom it was given to know his mystery. But this testimony could be transmitted to us only by successive generations of believers who in continuity with the apostles have lived their faith in the grace of the Spirit of Christ ever present in his Church. It is within this communion of all with all that it becomes possible for us to grasp with certitude the real meaning of the scriptures.

It is out of this unanimity of their faith that the people of faith announce the "Good News" they have received; it is the faith of a believing community that carries and supports our own individual faith. Indeed it is of the very nature of faith that it be lived only in the communion of all with all.

The reality of this communion gives profound significance to the meaning of obedience in the Church. Far beyond whatever submission to lawful authority may mean in the secular realm, in the Church it arises out of the very nature of faith. For faith as we have said can be lived only within the unanimity of believers, a unanimity safeguarded through witnesses who have received the mission to be its servants.

Since, therefore, there is no other way of living our faith than together, as one, our first concern must be to maintain our unity. This requires that we be prepared to yield in matters purely individual when these cannot be reconciled with the sense of faith matured throughout the life of the Church, a sense we have been called to share. Concern for unity, however, also means that we respect others, that we are open and understanding toward their way of living the truths central to our faith.

We have seen in this discussion how deeply our life is rooted in the life of the Church. We can receive our faith, on which everything rests, only in communion with the Church. The knowledge of so close a solidarity at the heart of our Christian life draws us to love the Church. Our highest good is to remain within its unity, sharing deeply in its life. For it is in the Church that Christ is present to us to make us one in him within the grace of his love.

*He who eats my flesh and drinks
my blood lives in me and I in him.
As I, who am sent by the living
Father, myself draw life from the
Father, so whoever eats me will draw
life from me.*　　　John 6:56-57

Chapter 5

THE SACRAMENT OF FAITH

The Eucharist is not merely a mystery of faith but *the* mystery of faith, the *Mysterium Fidei*. In the Eucharist is found the fullness of the revelation and of the gift God makes of himself in Jesus Christ.

Chapter 6 of St. John draws a parallel between our union with Christ through faith in his word and our union with him through sharing in his Body and Blood. The two are seen as inseparable, two aspects of one and the same incomparable mystery. Within that parallel is expressed the true character of faith: our intimate bond with Christ finding its full expression in the eucharistic meal. And this is what we wish to speak of now, the Eucharist as full expression of our faith.

Eucharist and faith

In the gospel faith is far more than intellectual adherence to a body of truths. It is a personal bond with Christ, a bond that commits us to him unreservedly. Those who have truly found and committed themselves to Christ can no longer live except for him, with him and in him. Henceforth they know only Christ and that they belong totally to the One to whom they have so given themselves. Nothing else exists for them: "If any man comes to me without hating his father, mother, wife, children, brothers, sisters, yes and his own life too, he cannot be my disciple" (Luke 14:26). It is necessary to be free of everything in order to be truly Christ's, following closely in his footsteps: "Whoever does not carry the cross and come after me, cannot be my disciple" (ibid., v. 27).

But if Christ wants his disciples to belong so entirely to him, it is to form with them a bond of such intimacy as to surpass any bond in this world uniting master and disciple. Our bond with Christ brings us into a world of realities completely divine. We are placed in the presence of him who comes to us as the "Entirely Other" to draw us in his infinite liberty so close as really and truly to give us a share in his life without in any way compromising his sovereignty.

In Chapter 17 of St. John's gospel we find the strongest statement of the relationship the disciple enters into with Christ to the point of becoming one with him: "That they may have my joy fulfilled in themselves . . . . I desire that where I am they also may be with me . . . . That the love with which you have loved me may be in them, and that I may be in them . . . . I have given them the glory you gave me, that they may be one as we are one, I in them and you in me, that they may be completely one."

This mystery of "what God has prepared for those who love him," a mystery that "no eye has seen, nor ear heard, nor the heart of man conceived" (1 Cor. 2:9) is nothing less than the mystery of a God inviting us to live in deepest intimacy with him. This mystery is the very object, the substance, of our faith, the gift bestowed on those who believe, for "whoever believes has eternal life." But it is expressed through the sign given us in the Eucharist: "As I, who am sent by the living Father, myself draw life from the Father, so whoever eats me will draw life from me" (John 6:47,57).

Eucharist and Incarnation

That God could admit us to such intimacy with himself as to bring us into the interchange of love that is his very life and in this love make us one with him—this is more than the human mind can imagine. Only a God incarnate could bring us to believe a mystery so

unbelievable. Only by his sharing our human condition
and living the mystery of his inmost life in a human
nature like ours could we come to believe ourselves called
to live his life with him, in the human condition that
is ours.

And to confirm our faith in so great a mystery, no
clearer sign could have been given us than the Eucharist.
What in truth does the action of the Eucharist signify? For
Christ to give himself as our food can only mean a true
communion of his life, a veritable gift of himself given us
that we may be made one with him.

The Eucharist reveals the true meaning of our faith:
the intimacy of the bond that in and through the
Eucharist we are given to live with Christ. The Eucharist
is the sign that enables us to accept this revelation, the
sign that makes it believable. He who drew so close to us
in the mystery of his Incarnation, who in the Eucharist
enables us to live this intimacy of God with each of
us—we can believe such a one when he reveals the
mystery of "what could not have entered the human
heart."

Eucharist and Redemption

In taking human flesh God entered our history to
deliver us from the sinfulness to which we were slaves, to
transform our history of sin into a history of salvation.

Christ saves us indeed by his entire life for his entire
life is inserted into our history and truly identified
with it. But the redeeming act *par excellence*, the central
act in the entire history of salvation, is the mystery of his
death and resurrection.

Because this redemptive sacrifice is for us the unique
source of all grace, Christ willed it to remain present to all
generations in order to carry and keep us in its grace.
Christ offered himself as victim for us all but also in token

of our oblation of ourselves. In offering himself he offered us too, inasmuch as we are one with him. That we ourselves might ratify this offering, however, it was necessary that this unique sacrifice remain present through time.

This is the meaning of the eucharistic sacrifice; it adds nothing to the one sacrifice of Christ. It does not even "repeat" it. It simply continues Christ's sacrifice in our history, making it really and truly present in every moment of this history under the sacramental sign he himself gave us.

The biblical notion of "memorial" emphasizes this aspect of the Eucharist. A memorial is the liturgical action in which the event being celebrated is not only commemorated but made present again; the participants live this event and draw from it the fruits of grace.

Only a divine intervention in history can be celebrated as a memorial, however. For although this intervention does indeed take place at a given moment in time it cannot be locked into any time limits. As an act of God it has the dimension of eternity: "Acts of God, though inserted in historical time through their contingent realization, nevertheless transcend time. The history of salvation moves to fulfillment in a perpetual actualization of what was, what is and will always remain, regardless of the flow of time and history."[3]

In sacred scripture the supreme memorial is the Passover Supper, Israel's celebration of the act of deliverance by which God made Israel his own people in becoming himself their Deliverer: "The Passover Supper did more than call to mind or evoke this event of the distant past. In and through the Passover Supper the event itself was to take on, each year, its full actuality for every generation, for all time to come."[4]

It is profoundly significant then that Christ instituted the memorial of the definitive act of deliverance—his death and resurrection—while celebrating the memorial of the act of deliverance that announced and prefigured his own, namely the exodus of Israel from Egypt.

The Eucharist is continuous presence—insertion into each moment of history—of the unique saving Act accomplished by Christ; continuous presence of this definitive Act in the life of the Church and in the life of each Christian. By means of the Eucharist Christ continually draws the Church and in her each Christian into the grace of this unique saving Act.

The Fourth Eucharist Prayer, by situating this saving Act within the successive stages in the history of salvation, reminds us that the event we are about to celebrate—the death and resurrection of Christ—takes us to the very heart of this history. And the double invocation of the Holy Spirit that frames the Prayer makes clear that we are about to do far more than recall this event—this we could do on our own. In and by our celebration this event will become truly present again, gathering us up in its grace. And that can be done only through the all-powerful intervention of the Holy Spirit.

Only in this perspective can we begin to grasp the full meaning and depth of our union with Christ in eucharistic communion. Under this sign Christ not only becomes our food but also brings us into his Sacrifice.

Those who "in the sacrificial meal" have presented the victim as sign of their own offering and consecration to God are nourished by this victim. This enables them to form a deeper union with Christ and to participate with him as consecrated victim.

In order to reconcile and consecrate humanity to his Father Christ offered us along with himself. We ratify this offering when we celebrate and partake of the Eucharist.

Eucharist and history of salvation

By drawing us into the presence of the central event of history the Eucharist reminds us that the Christian life is an involvement in this same history. Indeed the authentic meaning of our Christian life can be understood only in this perspective.

To enter in union with Christ into the mystery of his death and resurrection standing at the center of the history of salvation is to be inserted into this history, into the great river of grace flowing through it. It is to enter into communion with all who across space and time have lived or are living this history.

In this dynamic perspective our Christian life, our responsibility as Christians, takes on the fullness of meaning described by Father Yves Congar as each of us carrying a part of the history of salvation for the benefit of all.

To see the world as full of the mystery of grace present and carrying it along in its all-redeeming power is a new and deeply moving perspective. It teaches us to pursue our work in this world with an eagerness inspired and sustained by hope.

Eucharist and Eschatology

The Eucharist is essentially a mystery of hope. In it the plenitude toward which we are moving is already present. For the accomplishment of all things in Christ will be no other than the complete fulfillment of grace already contained whole and entire in the redemptive Sacrifice, unique source of our salvation. Carried along in the grace of this central mystery we move toward final fulfillment.

United with Christ the risen Head, sharing even now in his life as the Risen One, the Church in celebrating the Eucharist is already transported into the world to come.

As Professor Von Allmen has said, the Eucharist "in some way lifts the Church into the kingdom that is coming; it places the Church in the world of resurrection." In the eucharistic celebration there is "anticipation of the Parousia, regular confirmation of Salvation and a *gradual becoming accustomed to what the Kingdom will be.*"[5]

For the Church, to celebrate the Eucharist is to grow accustomed to the life of heaven and to strengthen our hope for it. "Lord Jesus, come. . . . We proclaim your death, until you come in glory . . . . We wait in joyful hope for the coming of our Savior, Jesus Christ." By calling us to voice this hope in the course of the eucharistic celebration the Church reminds us that we can live this central act of our Christian life only in the spirit of waiting and hoping for Christ's return. It is in this disposition that we must live our entire Christian life.

The Eucharist places us then in a perspective both historical and eschatological. The two are inseparable; for if history is to unfold its true meaning it must be seen in the light of the hope toward which it is tending.

A mystery of presence

These perspectives—historical and eschatological together—help to bring out the full meaning of the mystery of Christ's real presence in the Eucharist. In instituting the Eucharist Christ's primary concern was that his Sacrifice, unique source of salvation for the world, remain present to the entire history of the world, in order to carry it along in the grace of his Sacrifice. If he is present for us it is in the act of this Sacrifice wherein he is both Priest and Victim. He is present in the Eucharist then as a presence who acts. He is present there sustaining all history in the unique grace of his redemptive Sacrifice. He is present there building the Church, his Body, in the power of his own risen body. He is present there to the Church and, through the Church, to the world, accomplishing in and through her his work of salvation.

We have emphasized the link between the Eucharist and the Incarnation. When we profess faith in the real presence of Christ in the Eucharist, we profess faith in the plenitude of the mystery of the Incarnation: the role of Christ's humanity in the plan of salvation, in the work of the redemption of the world.

Christ died and rose that we might enter with him into the mystery of his death and resurrection (Romans 6). It is in the power of his own risen body that he builds his Body the Church and through the Church, a new world (Colossians 1). It is in uniting us with his risen body that he gives us even now a pledge of our own resurrection. And in uniting us with his humanity—with the body delivered for us, with the blood poured out for us—he gives us a share in his divinity.

The Incarnation is not God's coming on earth for some limited time only. It is God's definitive involvement in our history. Christ remains with us under the sign he himself has given us—his Church. At the heart of the Church's life is the Eucharist, the unique and incomparable mystery of Christ's presence among us. Not only the Eucharist, however, but the whole life of the Church in all its aspects is for us the expression of a presence that extends to every part of our life, carried along as it is within the life of the Church. The Christian mystery then is neither more nor less than the mystery of a presence of Christ. The Eucharist does indeed express and actualize the fullness of this presence, but the Eucharist itself is truly understood only in relation to a greater mystery of presence in the new reality of a world drawn by God into an intimate union through his Incarnation.

This understanding clarifies the significance of the mystery of the Church itself, its place in God's plan. To reject the Church is not merely to refuse obedience to an authority instituted by God. The offense goes much deeper to a rejection of the covenant of love. For in rejecting the Church we reject the mystery of the Incarnation in its fullness, the mystery of Christ's presence in our history under the signs he has given us—signs which belong to our history, which really and truly insert Christ's presence into it in order to draw that history into the Incarnation, the fullness of the covenant promise.

If any man is thirsty, let him come to me! Let the man come and drink who believes in me! From his breast shall flow fountains of living water.

Psalm 7:37-38

Chapter 6

LIVING A PRESENCE

To believe in this presence that surrounds us on all sides; to recognize it in every sphere of the Church's life; to discover it in each and all who in communion with the Church are for us its living signs, its 'sacraments': there can be no better help toward living this presence than attitudes like these.

It also touches each one of us in the very depths of our being like a deeply personal love. But often it seems to withdraw from us. In such seasons of absence we need to stir up our faith in the presence, in the great mystery, of this love that surrounds us on all sides.

When we feel ourselves unworthy of this love, and indeed especially then, we must remember it is in our very poverty that this love enfolds us all and carries us along. For it is not a privilege of which we are worthy or unworthy but rather a gift of grace that together we all receive. We must accept it in a humility that leads us on to loving acceptance and concern for all whom God loves with the same incomparable love.

My soul waits for the Lord more than watchmen for the morning.

Psalm 130:6

The mystery of God seems to lie beyond our comprehension. We can only reverence its secret, dwelling in silence before it. And yet, God reveals himself as wanting to draw us into intimate union with himself. How is this possible?

A God so near and yet so far away. We are nothing before him, yet he draws us into his very life.

Let us not imagine his mystery as shut away in incommunicable perfection infinitely beyond our reach. The mystery of God is wide openness, radiancy of his own splendor, enveloping and penetrating with his own light all who give themselves to the grace of his presence.

Only when we try to struggle upward to him by our own efforts does he seem to withdraw to regions forever beyond us.

If we simply open ourselves to his grace we will discover how near he is and with what dynamism of grace and love he lays hold of us, drawing us into intimate union with himself.

Simply to bathe in the radiancy of this mystery.
To be fully open before him
    in an act of faith in him
    in the humility of faith.

We cannot know God as he is. His mystery remains infinitely beyond our reach. Yet in a simple act of faith lies a glimmer of his plenitude, and even this glimmer is a very true, very deep way of knowing him. In this very act of faith we can discover and live a true intimacy with him.

An attitude of faith: the only attitude possible before
him, the only attitude that is true. No matter how
impoverished our prayer we may rest content, knowing
our prayer of faith opens on him who holds it up in his
grace: our prayer lived within an act of faith.

Not to look at ourselves: we will see
nothing but our poverty.
To look only at God:
    to allow him to find what he can
    in our poverty
        lived as a prayer of
        supplication to him.
To see only him
    him whom we believe
    him whom we adore
        in total surrender before him.

The Lord is present at the center and source of such
an attitude, an attitude completely open and uplifted
toward infinity, an attitude possible only before him and
only in and because of him.

It is truly he whom we encounter in
our heart of hearts.
To come to see ourselves in him is to
see only him.
We cannot see him
but if we have come to see everything
only in him
are we not seeing him always?

Teach me O Lord, your way that I may walk in your truth; direct my heart that it may fear your name.

Psalm 86:11

God's presence reaches to our inmost being: it makes us a new creation. For now we no longer exist except in a bond of love with him who is our deepest truth.

God's mystery infinitely distant is nevertheless infinitely near. Indeed we truly know ourselves only in knowing him who dwells in our heart of hearts.

A veiled presence, but we are pure affirmation of this presence. Everything in us testifies to it as giving us the truth of our being.

We live by this presence and only by it and we cannot lay hold on it. We can only lose ourselves in an act of faith in it that opens on infinity.

Not that the mind understands
        only the deepest recesses of our consciousness.
To receive his presence simply as a grace.
To live it freely.
To let ourselves be borne along in
this mystery of grace and love.
To be nothing but adoration
        silently   humbly.

To be simply under God's gaze the person he brings to being within us by the grace of his presence.

Peacefully   in simple assent.

To believe in God, to believe that in him we are all that we are, is to believe that within us exists a realm beyond what our mind can grasp. We can only be dimly aware of this and cling to it in faith.

Our very being, our truest self, when drawn into the mystery of grace cannot be confined to what our senses can perceive or follow.

Simply to be open to what the Lord
allows us to be
in him and with him.
To live thus in the freedom of faith
in his love.
An obscure movement of love at the
heart of an act of faith
in him whom we love
in him who we know loves us.
Through this movement of love   and   beyond
to live faith in this love
faith open on infinite love.

Our heart is never empty of love. Always it carries as its innermost truth the longing implanted in it by him who created us for his love. This love is not the fruit of our efforts. It precedes our efforts. It lives always secretly in our heart.

To assent to it
simply   freely.

Our deepest life can in no way be confined within human limits. It opens on the mystery of God carrying us along in the grace of his love, causing us to be all that we are.

A presence. In the measure we deepen our faith in the divine fullness of this presence, in the dynamism of grace and love into which it lifts us, in that measure will we come to a response that is simple, free.

Even before a word is on my tongue, behold, O Lord, you know the whole of it.

Psalm 139:4

The presence of a God who loves us. And who has loved us first. Our prayer rests on faith in a love that always anticipates and surpasses us.

God loves us with a true love. In his eyes we are not poor and empty. We are rich in that love whereby he has first loved us.

We are loved; we are caught up in the mystery of this love. In our loving union with him lies the deepest truth of our being.

Our attitude before God is true if it expresses our faith in what we really are before him, enfolded within that love.

Simply to be open to the infinite freedom of love
in serene faith in the love that
can read a response
in the silence of the heart.
To know how to live this response in
utter simplicity.
To offer to the Lord our faith in his love
the faith he enables us to live at
this present moment.

To let ourselves be stripped of everything and yet to believe firmly in what the Lord can bring to life in the heart of even the poorest of the poor.

To stand, even in our poverty, in the presence of so
great a mystery is of great worth.

Adoration lived as our deepest truth
    in a simplicity we can have before him alone
    in a simplicity that is reverence
    for his mystery
        humility in his presence.
Faith in what he can bring to life
    in the heart of even the most ordinary prayer.
To know we are loved with a love of compassion.
To know *everyone* is loved with a true
 love of predilection
    and so   more easily
to believe *oneself* loved with a love
of predilection.

When all seems lost there remains at least faith in a
love that cannot be deceived.

Let the hearts of those that seek the Lord rejoice.

Psalm 105:3

A presence that brings peace. However hidden it may be, we know that were it not there everything in us would be different.

From the heart of the most silent prayer can arise a delicate awareness that it is good for us to remain thus in stillness with the Lord, that in the depths of our silence lies something he alone can bring to life in the heart of an act of faith in him: herein lies the imperceptible transparency of grace.

To let ourselves be immersed in the grace of his presence: this is a grace bringing peace to our heart when all in us is silence and we are tempted to wonder if this silence is prayer.

At the heart of our prayer the *reality* of an ever-acting presence: this is the very truth of our prayer, beyond the realm of consciousness.

To come to recognize that we are changed imperceptibly yet profoundly because we believe in this presence.

It is in knowing we are in his hands that we can become truly simple.

Being simply what we are under his gaze
knowing *he* sees.

We know that the bond of true friendship is steadfast; it is not at the mercy of how we feel or what we experience at any given moment. We know that come what may the bond of love will endure.

To live aware of a steadfast bond with him before whom we are nothing, in whom we are all that we are: his presence is our inmost truth.

To remain under the gaze of him who
is always with us.
Never to see ourselves as other than
under this gaze.
Never to see ourselves as simply
ourselves, existing apart from him.
To stand before God as we are in the
abiding grace of his love.
To remain in the radiancy of his presence
acting within us.
To offer ourselves to this grace.
To build nothing ourselves.

In the presence of the Lord let us simply live our
truest self: the silent adoration that lies in the depths of
our heart.

This presence can never fail us. If it fades or seems
to fade we need not go in anxious search for signs of it; we
need only renew our faith in it.

To be absolutely trusting
    (the gaze of the Lord on him who
    believes in his love
        who humbly trusts him).
To be humble   docile
    in faith before him
        in complete openness.
This attitude alone is true.

O Lord, my heart is not proud, nor are my eyes haughty; I busy not myself with great things, nor with things too sublime for me. Nay, rather, I have stilled and quieted my soul like a weaned child. Like a weaned child on its mother's lap, so is my soul within me.

Psalm 131:1-2

A presence drawing the most profound depth of our being into openness toward a mystery infinitely greater than we are. Yet everything in us mirrors it.

Simply to be open to what another brings to life in our heart, knowing only that without him we cannot live, without him who created us to live by his love.

Our entire being is a call toward him. Pure call. To be just that under his gaze is to be our truest self.

To rest in an attitude of truth
in the simplicity of faith
accepting its darkness.

The mystery of God is mirrored in our attitude before him, is deeply present in our silences, cannot be contained within any thought of ours.

To let the Lord shape us to his likeness by awakening in us an attitude of truth in his presence.

Simply who we are because we believe
in his presence.
No longer existing except in an act
of faith in him
No longer anything but faith in him

If in our heart of hearts there lies a yearning greater than the heart, it is because that One exists toward whom the yearning tends and nothing escapes the radiancy of his light. Because he exists we are who we are, pure call toward him.

Our part is simply to acquiesce, to receive from
another what we are in him and through him.
   To reverence this mystery.
   Not to doubt it   it is not our doing
      it does not depend at all on our
      poor and fragile being.

   In the depths of our consciousness a pure act of faith
opening on an infinity beyond the limits of our thought.
   Pure silence in the presence of the infinite, allowing
it to overflow our human limits: this is pure adoration.
   Silence filled with a presence.
   Silence lived always open to this presence.
   Silence become true prayer.

   To accept having absolutely nothing of our own:
our prayer exists only thanks to him who can understand
it, who can read in the depths of our heart what we can
only babble.
   He alone knows the secret of our inmost selves;
he brings this secret to life in us as a gift.
   Simply an assent to it
      an assent that is our deepest truth.

The desire of the afflicted you hear,
O Lord.

Psalm 10:17

Faith in a love ever present, a love that carries us in its grace, that anticipates and makes possible our slightest movement toward it. This faith can be expressed only in the freedom of simplicity.

To live in the presence of God is to be open in the freedom of simplicity to the dynamism of his love giving itself in infinite freedom, always alive.

The only true attitude in the presence of this mystery of divine graciousness: the freedom of simplicity, a genuine emptying of self.

Humility enables us to live freely our trust in him for whom our poverty is no obstacle: the most ordinary prayer opens us to his grace freely given.

A humble silence can by itself express
who we are before him.
To be pure contemplation
open to his plenitude infinitely
above and beyond us
open to what is given us to
glimpse of this plenitude.

Everything that speaks to us of God, however delicately, opens on his infinity. That is enough to turn us toward him, open us to his grace in simple assent.

A deep will to be attentive to God, to be open to him: however delicately it is expressed, he hears and accepts.

To believe in the reality of our prayer even when we can no longer see clearly within ourselves is to believe in the fidelity of Love always present to what he brings to life however secretly in our heart.

A true act of faith in him.
Him we cannot doubt
nor his mercy.
A true surrender of all that is of ourselves
before him who carries us   *all together*
in the grace of his love.

True simplicity is utter openness to God, to his grace freely given, in a surrender of our whole selves before him. It is utter humility. It is an act of faith.

If we really believe in the plenitude of a love that is the very mystery of God and in the profundity of his embrace reaching to the very depths of our being, we will be all simplicity in his presence.

A humble simplicity that opens us to him.
An attitude of truth before him.
True progress in love: to become more
humble before him.

Our prayer exists only in relation to the One before whom it is complete openness and complete assent. Only in turning toward him does our prayer discover itself.

The simplest prayer, however poor, takes on meaning in the light of the One on whom its gaze has come to rest.

It is enough to know that he exists. For it is from him that a simple gaze receives the plenitude of existence and of truth.

My soul longs, yea faints for the courts of the Lord; my heart and flesh sing for joy to the living God.

Psalm 84:2

Faith in the presence of a love infinitely free to give itself moves us to live a hope that knows no limits. It opens on a mystery surpassing our comprehension.

Aware that we cannot live without him, that we live in him a hope that rests on him alone.

A simple desire to be freely open to him over and above any desire we might have as our own.

A simple openness to his desire to give himself to us.

An assent to what the Lord brings to life in our heart freely, by his grace.

Living by our faith in him
      leaving everything in his hands.

If in true surrender of ourselves before God we place our trust in him alone, all our desires are uplifted into a realm surpassing hope.

If we really understood who it is on whom our hope rests, how serenely we would live a wholehearted desire to be docile to him.

To judge a longing for God by the intensity of its feeling would be to consider this longing as our own and thus to confine it within human limitations.

A humble openness to the love of God lived in the darkness of faith is openness to his love given with infinite freedom.

What the Lord brings to life in the depths of our
heart: that is our deepest truth.

To live it freely   through every darkness
        in faith in him
                in the faithfulness of his love.

When we no longer find anything but emptiness in
ourselves, to recognize the secret intimations of faith in
our heart.

The mystery hidden there
        the mystery of love
        the mystery of a presence carrying
        us in its grace.

We open ourselves to this mystery by an assent of
faith that is our deepest truth.

Not to confine it within our human limits.
To receive it   simply as it is given.
To be utterly open to the Lord
        pure assent to his love infinitely free
        in simplicity born of humility.

To pray is to live in a realm above and beyond our
prayer, for everything in us that is prayer opens on this
infinity.

Because faith makes us completely open to the
infinity of God, it lifts us into a new reality, a realm
beyond the finite where all human limitations disappear.

Our hope must be freely open to this infinity with no
thought of falling back on ourselves.

The Lord is merciful and gracious, slow to anger and abounding in steadfast love. He does not deal with us according to our sins, nor requite us according to our iniquities.

Psalm 103:8,10

Faith in love is true only if everything gives way
before the assurance that we can hope for all things
from the plenitude of this love.

Absolute assent to what lies deepest in our heart
secretly present to all that we are.

Secretly   a grace
      lived freely   humbly.

What lies deepest in our heart is a presence we are
open to but are unable to lay hold on, an active presence.

If we truly believe in the divine fullness of the mystery
that carries us in its grace, we will even under the most
ordinary circumstances recognize its presence and be able
to live it.

Prayer is an attitude of truth before God. The more it
recognizes and accepts itself as poor, the truer it is. And
the more truly it is prayer.

Grace lived in the heart of an attitude of prayer
before God: simply to allow ourselves to be permeated by
this grace.

Faith is assent. What it glimpses of the mystery is
expressed in this assent.

To entrust to the Lord the deepest longing of our
heart: he alone knows how this desire always reaching
beyond itself, always desiring more, will be fulfilled in
himself.

Faith in his love brings us into a world where all
measurements are dissolved and all limits are surpassed.

Simply not to close ourselves off from him by closing
ourselves off from love of neighbor.

Whatever our weaknesses, as soon as a desire for God arises in us God sees only this desire and uses it as an excuse to give us his grace. Then we too see only this grace, always present to help us overcome our weaknesses peacefully and in confidence.

Never to see ourselves as alone.
Never to believe ourselves abandoned
      cut off from his love.

What lies deepest in our heart is gift and grace. It is the radiancy of a presence in us. All lies in our being open to this presence, allowing it to act freely within us instead of straining in an anxious effort to accomplish by ourselves a work that would be only our own and that others would find inadequate.

Simple assent to what is deepest and truest in ourselves freely lived as a grace, open to the infinite fullness of a divine mystery of love.

"Yes" lived as a grace
      freely   in true simplicity.

The Lord sees what his grace brings to life in the most secret recesses of our heart.

Thou hast said, "Seek ye my face."
My heart says to thee, "Thy face,
Lord, do I seek." Hide not thy face
from me.

Psalm 27:8-9

The Lord is present in the heart of the simplest act of faith in his presence.

Faith, however imperfect it may be, remains a true encounter with the Lord in the measure that it is received as a gift. To recognize that we cannot claim it as ours alone is to perceive in it the presence of him who brings it to life in our heart.

Our faith has matured within us not simply as the fruit of our own reflections; we have not lived it alone. It has formed and deepened little by little under the stirring of a presence, the presence of him who loved us first and who draws us into the mystery of his love by living it within us.

This presence allows itself to be dimly felt in the heart of faith.

In the degree that faith is lived as a gift it unfolds into a boundless hope, an intimation of him who is already giving himself within the faith he brings to life in us.

Because this is an attitude we can have only before God there lives within it a kind of reflection of his mystery, of his plenitude.

If we recognize faith as a gift we will live it freely in true simplicity, able to perceive it always present in our silences.

In its light, which dispels the shadows of human thoughts and feelings, we will see all things. And we will give unceasing thanks.

To live our faith calmly and serenely, even when we
are no longer sure of anything except that someone is
there to receive it, to recognize it alive in the heart of our
darkness.

If only we knew who it is in whose presence we are,
how he looks on us.

To see ourselves only under this gaze
     open to him who enables us to live
          carrying us in the grace of a
          living communion.

Faith, however ordinary, and perhaps the more
ordinary it is, is the expression of truly belonging to God
alone: to live the mystery of this belonging as a grace
whose fullness surpasses anything we can imagine.

To live a mystery.
     Not trying to penetrate its secret   but
          to be open to the grace of its presence
          acting secretly within us.
To be open to it by a simple assent.
To live without clear knowledge of it   but
     to believe in it
     to be humbly submissive to it.

A mystery we can only dimly grasp. But this
intimation in the heart of an act of faith is true.

My soul thirsts for God, for the living God.

Psalm 42:2

To live freely the grace of a presence. In truth before
it. Utterly open to the hidden grace of this presence.

The mystery of God's presence is too deeply
implanted within us not to be alive in the heart of our
silences, even the most empty. It is our deepest truth,
received and lived as a grace in utter simplicity.

Our deepest truth, open on the infinity of God,
receives from it a dimension of infinity. All we can do is
live it.

If only we truly believed in the divine mystery
carrying us along in the grace of its ever acting presence,
we would learn to live our humble silence as a pure act of
faith.

A humble silence
truest expression of who we are
before him
poorest of the poor
in the plenitude of hope.

A mystery: we cannot better express our intimation
of it than by an ever deeper surrender of ourselves. Such
self-surrender is a way of being more open to him, in
greater truth before him.

To live freely our faith in his love: true love cannot
but have its demands. But he knows our weakness, our
frailty. When we humbly acknowledge our weakness we
stand before him in an attitude of truth, peacefully
committing to his mercy our desire to be freely open to
him.

Not to be deterred by the seeming poverty of our prayer but to believe in the fullness of the mystery our prayer opens on, a mystery carrying us in its grace.

We can sense that our prayer is deeper and truer than it looks. Its inmost truth is seldom apparent, but we can sense it in the depth of our heart.

At the heart of this inward prayer: the presence of him who calls it forth.

The heart tends toward him who is continually beyond us yet intimately present, because the heart is in its every fiber an aspiration toward him. It exists only as call toward him.

We cannot know ourselves unless we know him.

Only as in him can we know ourselves.

He is no stranger.

He is very near.

It is in our heart that we meet him, Someone infinitely beyond us yet one to whom we are utter openness.

For you, O Lord, are good and forgiving, abounding in kindness to all who call upon you. Hearken, O Lord, to my prayer and attend to the sound of my pleading.

Psalm 86:5-6

Simply to be open to him who is always with us.

Simply to live what the Lord continues to be to us in
the depth of our heart, even when that seems to have
vanished and we no longer perceive it remaining alive
deep down in our heart in spite of all the silences.

Secret adoration of his infinite fullness
        who frees us from all that is not himself
            from ourselves and our self-seeking.
A humble abandonment into his hands.

What is written very deep in our heart can be lived
quite simply. It is present in our simplest self-awareness,
permeating it imperceptibly.

What is most profound in us cannot be measured by
our feelings, by what reaches our clear consciousness.

It is more hidden because more true.

The pure simplicity of an attitude of acceptance: a
free openness to him who gives himself to us secretly in
the infinite freedom and mysterious fullness of his love.

What he brings to life in our heart can only be
perceived in the above and beyond of an act of faith.

There is no question of laying hold on it but of being
open to it.

To know the Lord better is to become more true
before him. To be more true is to be more simple, with a
simplicity showing that in all humility our hope rests in
him alone.

To be divested of all, no longer having anything
except our faith in him: this is true purity of heart suffused
in his light.

"Blessed are the pure in heart for they shall see God."

If we truly knew who it is in whom we believe, how
simply we could put our faith in him even when that faith
is deeply hidden in the most secret recesses of our heart.

God alone knows what he brings to life in the heart
of an act of faith. He enables us to know it clearly enough
to realize we could not live without him.

We need to be able to turn freely to him. If something
within us is in the way we cannot find peace again until
we have removed the obstacle.

That is why we need to be at peace with everyone.

We need to believe in his mercy. He sees the sincerity
of our desire and has pity on our weakness humbly
acknowledged before him.

To you, even silence is praise.

Psalm 65:2   Hebrew

Living a presence. To be before the Lord the person
we become each day in the grace of his presence.

A simplicity that speaks of God's simplicity. Humble
adoration of this simplicity: the only true attitude in his
presence.

Simply to be before the Lord the person
he enables us to be in his presence.
Receiving this from him with thanksgiving.
An assent to a reality of grace   a living reality.
Open to it without trying to encompass it
in our mind.

Little by little, living in a communion with him who
is always with us, we have become who we are. *All this
rests with him.* We need only turn toward him in order to
live what we have become before him.

To have in his presence an attitude that expresses
what he is for us, an intimation we can feel in the heart of
our communion with him, an intimation open to the
secret plenitude of what we are receiving as a grace.

An attitude of truth lived under his
gaze   in free simplicity.
An attitude more than merely the fruit
of our thoughts
        not depending on them.
A simple assent to what we are
        carried along in its grace
        above and beyond what we can surmise.

To stand before the Lord gazing simply at him: our attitude in his presence receives its truth from him.

The simple acceptance of a silence that no longer seems even a prayer can be the expression of this attitude of truth, a way of living what remains secretly present in the depth of this apparent void.

He who sees to the bottom of our heart can find there a true attitude of acceptance arising out of utter confidence.

Any work of ours would have merely human dimensions.

What we truly live as a grace surpasses all human measurement. We can only accept it, freely giving thanks.

Thanksgiving: a reverence for God's grace expressed in our freedom from dependence on all lesser things.

As for me, all in me is prayer.

Psalm 109:4

By the grace of his presence he makes our whole being a prayer.

To accept the seeming poverty of our prayer, to stand completely open in humble readiness to what remains hidden from us: that is to recognize the truth of the relationship that prayer enables us to live with God. It is an act of faith in him who enables our prayer to be fully itself yet in a realm above and beyond itself, in a communion with the mystery of him from whom it receives its inmost truth.

He alone knows the secret of the call he brings to life in our heart of hearts. He alone knows how he is already answering it by enabling us to live a true communion with him deep within this call—within his seeming absence.

To be simply and utterly what we are: pure assent to God, pure call to him. Therein lives our real truth; it subsists only in him, borne along in his grace.

A tending of our whole being toward God, even before the free assent by which we give ourselves to him.

A belonging to God alone that deepens our sense of being in his trust, of being able to do nothing except remain simply in his hands.

An abandonment into his hands that enables us to live the joy of belonging to him.

Plain and ordinary though it may be, a prayer arising out of our deepest, most hidden truth.

However ordinary it appears, may everything in us have already become prayer.

To live more and more spontaneously the knowledge that we receive our prayer from him who alone knows its secret
> the secret of his love
>> glimpsed only in his light.

To reverence this secret is to be humble in his presence. It is to find the ultimate truth of prayer in a realm above and beyond prayer: in him in whom it is all that it is—a living communion with him.

And those who know thy name put their trust in thee, for thou, O Lord, hast not forsaken those who seek thee.

Psalm 9:10

The intimation of a presence, open on the
transcendency of the mystery.

Every genuine turning toward God, however poorly
it is expressed, brings us into the mystery of his presence
and opens us to its grace.

A simple gaze toward God, an attitude that is all
that it is simply because we are in his presence: living it by
a simple assent we open ourselves to the grace always
deepening this presence within us.

We know we can trust everything to the Lord, above
all this attitude by which we express our faith in him.
That is why we can live our faith very simply.

To receive humbly whatever the Lord permits us to
glimpse of his mystery, knowing it is always infinitely
above and beyond.

To love the Lord with a love open on this
transcendency dimly perceived in the heart of an attitude
of truth in his presence

a glimpse expressible not in words   but
only in love.

In the humility of love   a gaze of love
in the silence of faith open to grace.

Not to confine the mystery of God to what we
can only dimly perceive.

To live this intimation open to its plenitude,
respecting its mystery, a respect expressed by the absolute
of our assent.

When we no longer know whether we love God, we know at least that at the heart of this attitude of respect we will find again the awareness that we love him.

To believe in what lives in our heart because we believe in the love that, as long as we do not purposely close ourselves off from it, cannot withhold itself from us.

Freely to live our faith in the love with
which we are loved.
To believe utterly in the infinite freedom
of God's love.
To reverence the *mystery* of his infinite freedom
of his mercy.
To live a hope that rests on him alone
when all else fails.

To accept in true simplicity what the Lord allows us to experience in a gaze towards him.

To receive it from him just as he
gives it   peacefully
a mystery of grace.
To live it in faith
in communion with all   together
in our poverty
carried along in a common mystery of grace.

To be liberated enough from ourselves to be open— simply, in a pure attitude of acceptance—to whatever grace brings to life in us: this is the freedom of children, the freedom of trustfulness.

*For a day in thy courts is better
than a thousand elsewhere.*

Psalm 84:10

An indwelling presence.

A simple gaze of faith.

It is enough to remember in whose presence we are.
Our attitude in his presence receives its truth from him.
All that it is, it is in him.

If we are truly aware of living a relationship with
God we will not be surprised that we must live it in
humble simplicity, in reverence for his mystery.

The gaze of the Lord on an attitude truly humble
in his presence.

To be before the Lord as one upon whom he can
look with a look of mercy, one who stands humbly under
his gaze.

Our deepest self is never empty. It is there that
grace is always present and acting. To accept this deepest
self is to open ourselves to this active presence.

This is the most instinctive movement of our heart.
It does not come from us. It simply is. We can only assent
to it in an act of thanksgiving.

To receive it truly   as a gift.

Never to see our attitude in prayer simply in itself
but as presented to God's gaze. Who knows what he sees
in this prayer, poor though it is? He can read it in our
heart, comprehend its silence.

The mystery of his gaze toward us. The mystery of
being allowed to stand in the light of this gaze
    in its profound mystery.
    To learn to commit to the Lord our faith itself.
    To live it under his gaze
        just as it is
        open to his grace   humbly.

A simple knowledge of ourselves: to know how to
recognize that what we seek is already secretly present
within us. It is indeed our deepest self.
    To know we are in him who is always with us.
    All rests on him   on his presence.
    All is faith in his presence.
    To reverence the mystery of God and his presence
is the secret of true simplicity in prayer.
    In reverencing this mystery we can recognize its
presence hidden in the heart of our silences, in the heart
of our most ordinary prayer.

I cry out in the night before thee.
Let my prayer come before thee.
Psalm 88:1-2

It is by advancing along the purifying way of
renunciation that faith is deepened.

To the mystery of a God so near, carrying us in the
grace of a living communion with him, the only fitting
response is simple faith in the mystery of this ever acting
presence.

To believe in the presence of God as in the presence
of an infinite dynamism of grace and love.

Living his secret presence in a pure act of faith in
him is to live a very intimate bond of love with him.

To live peacefully the joy of a hope that rests on God
alone, in faith in his love freely given and in faith in its
plenitude manifested in each of the mysteries of our faith.

Nothing can limit our hope when we stand in the
presence of a love before which we can be only openness,
humble acceptance.

Humble acceptance in faith carries us beyond human
limits, opens us to the liberty of grace.

If we truly stand in the presence of the Lord, all
thought of our human limits will vanish in the adoration
of his unfathomable plenitude.

Faith enables us to live the plenitude perceivable in
the depths of an utter simplicity where nothing limits it.
This is the truest image we can have of God. Every act of
renunciation is an act of faith in this unique plenitude.

If we are mindful that together we receive everything in the poverty common to all, the other will no longer be the "other."

And we can no longer live anything simply as our own.

Not to want an extraordinary prayer but to want to be really poor before God: this is what opens us to his grace.

To open our heart to the grace of loving what remains hidden to us.

If only we knew what grace brings to life in our heart of hearts even when we are no longer aware of it; our silences can no longer be entirely empty.

What we are by our bond with Christ in the grace of his presence: it is enough to believe in this, to believe in what he brings to life in the most secret recesses of our heart, and to assent to it in utter simplicity.

This act of faith lies at the heart of prayer.

The Eucharist is the sign that enables us to live freely our faith in the presence, within even our humblest prayer, of this great mystery: the mystery of our living communion with Christ.

Knowing ourselves loved.

To know ourselves loved
    with a love of mercy
        that loves us in our poverty.

    The One whom we glimpse in the heart
of our attitude of truth before him.
    Our inmost self speaks of him and
speaks only of him. Hence this witness: he is the
One and All.

    The mystery of our belonging to God.
    A mystery that is our inmost truth.
    To assent to it   a simple assent.
    To be pure assent.

    An ordinary prayer lived as a pure
    attitude of acceptance.
    Prayer in every way like the poorest of the
    poor
        open on a realm above and beyond its
        poverty
        open on the simplicity of God
            the freedom of his love
            its infinite plenitude
        open on a hope without limits.

Our truest self
    lived as a grace.
An attitude of truth before God:
    a simplicity that is pure humility.
An attitude we can have only before him:
    pure adoration.

A humble assent to what can only be
received
    in the silence of faith.
To live under the gaze of God an attitude of
truth
    opening us to his grace.

NOTES

1. Gustave Martelet, for example, has expressed himself to this effect. See also his study, *The Risen Christ and the Eucharistic World.* Translation (New York: Seabury Press, 1977).

2. Max Thurian. (Efforts to track down this reference proved futile. —Trans.)

3. F. J. Leenhardt, "Ceci est mon corps." Translated in *Essays on the Lord's Supper* (Richmond: John Knox Press, 1958).

4. J. Bonsirven, *Textes Rabbiniques*, 868 (Rome, 1955).

5. J. J. Von Allmen, "Essai sur le repas du Seigneur," *Cahiers Theologiques* 55.